Pebble Bilingual Books

Soy responsable/ I Am Responsible

de/by
Sarah L. Schuette

Traducción/Translation
Martín Luis Guzmán Ferrer, Ph.D.

Capstone Press
Mankato, Minnesota

Pebble Bilingual Books are published by Capstone Press
151 Good Counsel Drive, P.O. Box 669, Mankato, Minnesota 56002
http://www.capstone-press.com

Printed in the United States of America

1 2 3 4 5 6 08 07 06 05 04 03

Library of Congress Cataloging-in-Publication Data
Schuette, Sarah L., 1976–
    [I am responsible. Spanish & English]
    Soy responsable / de Sarah L. Schuette; traducción, Martín Luis Guzmán Ferrer =
I am responsible / by Sarah L. Schuette; translation, Martín Luis Guzmán Ferrer.
        p. cm.—(Pebble bilingual books)
    Spanish and English.
    Includes index.
    Summary: Simple text and photographs show various ways children can be
responsible.
    ISBN 0-7368-2306-9
    1. Responsibility—Juvenile literature. [1. Responsibility. 2. Spanish language
materials—Bilingual.] I. Title: I am responsible. II. Title. III. Series: Pebble bilingual
books.
BJ1451 .S33818 2004
179'.9—dc21   2003004953

Credits
Mari C. Schuh and Martha E. H. Rustad, editors; Jennifer Schonborn, book designer
    and illustrator; Patrick Dentinger, cover production designer; Gary Sundermeyer,
    photographer; Nancy White, photo stylist; Karen Risch, product planning editor;
    Eida Del Risco, Spanish copy editor; Gail Saunders-Smith, consulting editor;
    Madonna Murphy, Ph.D., Professor of Education, University of St. Francis, Joliet,
    Illinois, author of *Character Education in America's Blue Ribbon Schools*, consultant

Pebble Books thanks the Mankato Family YMCA of Mankato, Minnesota, and the
Bacon family of North Mankato, Minnesota, for their assistance with this book. The
author dedicates this book to her grandmother, Minnie L. Simcox, of Belle Plaine,
Minnesota.

Table of Contents

Responsibility 5
At Home 7
In the Community 17
Glossary 22
Index/Word List 24

Contenido

La responsabilidad 5
En el hogar 7
En la comunidad 17
Glosario 23
Índice 24

4

I am responsible. I do what I should do.

Yo soy responsable. Hago lo que debo hacer.

I feed my goldfish.

Les doy de comer
a mis pececitos.

8

I make my bed
every morning.

Hago mi cama
todos los días.

I brush my teeth.

Me lavo los dientes.

I help my dad
dry the dishes.

Ayudo a mi papá
a secar los platos.

I practice for
my piano lesson.

Practico mi lección
de piano.

I get to
swimming lessons
on time.

Llego puntual a
mis clases de natación.

I bring my supplies
to school.

Llevo mis útiles
a la escuela.

People can depend on me. I am responsible.

Las personas pueden contar conmigo. Soy responsable.

Glossary

depend—to count on someone to do the right thing

piano—a large musical instrument with white keys and black keys; people press the keys to make music on the piano.

practice—to work in order to learn a skill

responsible—doing what you say you will do; people who are responsible keep promises and follow rules.

supplies—materials needed to do something; school supplies include notebooks, pencils, and crayons.

Glosario

contar (con alguien)—saber que una persona hará las cosas correctamente

piano—gran instrumento musical con teclas blancas y teclas negras; la persona presiona las teclas para crear música.

practicar—tratar de avanzar en un conocimiento

responsable—cumplir con lo que digo que voy a hacer; las personas responsables cumplen con su palabra y con las reglas.

útiles—materiales necesarios para hacer algo; los útiles escolares incluyen cuadernos, lápices y crayones.

Index

bed, 9
bring, 19
brush, 11
dad, 13
depend, 21
dishes, 13
dry, 13
every, 9

feed, 7
goldfish, 7
help, 13
lesson, 15, 17
make, 9
morning, 9
people, 21
piano, 15

practice, 15
responsible,
   5, 21
school, 19
supplies, 19
swimming, 17
teeth, 11
time, 17

Índice

ayudo, 13
cama, 9
clases, 17
comer, 7
contar, 21
días, 9
dientes, 11
escuela, 19
hago, 9

lavo, 11
lección, 15
llevo, 19
natación, 17
papá, 13
pececitos, 7
personas, 21
piano, 15
platos, 13

practico, 15
puntual, 17
responsable,
   5, 21
secar, 13
todos, 9
útiles, 19